Bedfordshire at Work

IN OLD PHOTOGRAPHS

NIGEL LUTT

RECORD OFFICE

Bedfordshire

County Council

ALAN SUTTON PUBLISHING LIMITED

Alan Sutton Publishing Limited
Phoenix Mill · Far Thrupp · Stroud
Gloucestershire · GL5 2BU

First published 1994
in association with the County Record Office,
Bedfordshire County Council

Cover photograph: The staff of R.V. Dove's,
Queen Street, Bedford, 1930s.

British Library Cataloguing in Publication Data.
A catalogue record for this book is available from
the British Library.

ISBN 0-7509-0786-X

Typeset in 9/10 Sabon.
Typesetting and origination by
Alan Sutton Publishing Limited.
Printed in Great Britain by
Ebenezer Baylis, Worcester.

To Ruth and Bhaksho

The Bedfordshire farm labourer.
Billy Wiggins, shown here
threshing beans with a flail in
about 1892, lived in Pavenham all
his life and was a tenant of College
Farm at the time of the 1891
census. He died in September
1910, aged eighty-three.

Contents

William and Mary Linger of Spring Lane, Stagsden, making lace, *c.* 1905. They worked for Tom Coombs, a Bedford draper who employed lace-workers on piece-rates in forty-nine local villages.

Introduction

A Londoner was once asked what sprang to mind when she thought of Bedfordshire and she immediately replied, 'Bricks, brussels sprouts, beer – and of course, pillow lace'. While there is some truth in the remark, this volume aims to put the record straight by showing the whole range of work carried out by Bedfordshire people in the century up to the early 1960s.

The photographs in this book came from the collections held by Bedfordshire Record Office, founded in 1913 as the first of what is now a network of county repositories across England and Wales. In the early years of the record office the emphasis was on the collection and preservation of documents for research of all kinds, and we only began to acquire local illustrations in significant numbers in the 1950s. By the 1960s there was increasing interest in old pictures, an interest partly fuelled by demolition of entire localities and the disappearance of old industries, and we were kindly loaned many old photographs for copying, which were then added to our collections as a permanent record. At present we have well over 100,000 images and we are always interested in adding to the collection.

While I was compiling this book it became apparent that photographs and documents complement each other in important ways. The earliest picture in this volume was taken by the Toddington antiquarian William Cooper-Cooper who photographed local gamekeeper Norman Snoxell with a poacher in about 1854. Not only is this an interesting photograph in its own right, but the documentary evidence available from other sources adds greatly to our knowledge. The diary of John Thomas Brooks of Flitwick tells us that Cooper-Cooper received his photographic apparatus from London on 25 May 1853, while the Toddington parish register informs us that Norman Snoxell was buried on 30 June 1855, aged seventy-three. This is one of the most rewarding types of research – when photographs and documentary evidence shed light on each other.

Photographs of people at work are scarce. When the first commercial photographers came to Bedfordshire in the late 1850s and early 1860s they naturally concentrated on satisfying the large demand for portrait photographs and general town views. They were not interested in creating a social record. The bulk of the photographs in this volume date from the 1890s onwards, when photography became more commonplace and families started to take or to commission photographs of their relatives at work. At the same time local firms awoke to the publicity value of photography and produced illustrated leaflets and commemorative booklets.

Many of the photographs reveal some element of 'stage management' on the part of the photographer, thanks partly to technological limitations imposed by long exposure times and the tendency of people to pose for the camera. Nevertheless, there is a great contrast between these vivid images of the past and the examples of romanticized engravings and paintings of people at work which occur before the age of photography. I have included a few of these views – the itinerant dealers in Dunstable ware, 1796, the Henlow enclosure surveyors of *c.* 1798 and the country couple from the Blunham enclosure map of 1799 – to demonstrate this contrast. The camera can mislead, even lie, but only up to a point.

If photographs of people at work are scarce, some particular views are very rare indeed. Photographers concentrated on busy scenes involving machinery and implements, animals, or road vehicles, and the more mundane activities of working life were often ignored. The photographs of Mary Ball of Pavenham washing up at her sink in 1896 and of the office clerks at George Kent of Luton, *c.* 1914, are probably unique views in our collections.

Bedfordshire has always been primarily an agricultural county and this is reflected in the first section, 'On the Land'. Among the more general views of threshing and sheep tending there are pictures of more localized activities. For example, market gardening has been important in central and east-central Bedfordshire since at least the seventeenth century, while the Aylesbury prune was grown at Billington, Stanbridge, Totternhoe and Eaton Bray until the 1960s.

The development of the local railway network between 1837 and 1872 opened new markets to the farmer and manufacturer alike and this speeded the development of manufacturing industries (see section 2) in the second half of the century. To take just one example, the numerous small brick kilns which had existed in the earlier part of the nineteenth century gradually gave way to the large firms concentrated near the railway lines. Another trend is also discernible in that some London-based firms moved to new sites in Bedfordshire: W.H. Allen, engineers, to Bedford in 1893–4, Vauxhall Motors (Luton, 1905), George Kent, meter manufacturers (Luton, 1908) and Meltis, confectioners (Bedford, 1913).

Hand in hand with the development of communications and manufacturing, and a steady rise in population from 108,000 in 1841 to 172,000 in 1901, came the growth of retailing (section 3, 'Who Will Buy . . . ?') and service industries (section 4, 'At Your Service'). At the same time cottage industries (see section 5) such as lace-making, basket-making, mat-making and straw-plaiting declined and had virtually disappeared by the end of the 1930s.

The two world wars had a similar impact on Bedfordshire as they did elsewhere, in that women largely replaced men called up to serve in the forces. The pictures in 'A Woman's Work . . . ' (section 6) show the impact of this change, the views of women doing domestic chores giving way to pictures of wartime labour ranging from working on airship fabric and street cleaning to bus driving and engineering.

An individual's working life was seldom all work; it was occasionally punctuated by incidents such as staff outings, accidents and unemployment. Some people, such as poachers and tramps, opted out of a regular working life altogether. The concluding section ('Odd Jobs and Time Off') covers this mixed bag of activities.

I hope that you will enjoy this book which contains some of the very finest pictures of people at work from the Bedfordshire Record Office collections. Our thanks go to the many people who have donated or loaned us photographs over the years and have made this volume possible.

Nigel Lutt
Bedfordshire Record Office

SECTION ONE

On the Land

The rural idyll as depicted in a cartouche from the Blunham enclosure map of 1799. The artist was probably John Goodman Maxwell who, with Thomas Thorpe, prepared the map.

WORKMEN'S NAMES	Week ending April 1889 SATURDAY 8	MONDAY 9	TUESDAY 10	WEDNESDAY 11	THURSDAY 12	FRIDAY 13
Geo. Tysoe	Thrashing	Thrashing	Mending Rails	Thrashing	Thrashing	Dressing
Robt. Tysoe	+	+	+	+	+	+
J. Hide	Dressing	Dressing	Dressing	+	+	Dung Co
M. Lacey	+	+	+	+	+	+
J. Hurdick	Th. Beans	Th. Beans	Wall	+	+	+
Bartram	Sheep	Sheep	Sheep	Sheep	Sheep	Sheep
C. Aspley	Plough	Plough	Oakley St	Thrashing	Thrashing	Joby
J. Hardick	Dressing	Dressing	+	+	+	3/4 Dung
H. Cox	Plough	Plough	Plough	—	—	Dung Ca
R. Tysoe	Clapham	Spring Straw	Spring Straw	Thrashing	Thrashing	+
J. Hide	Shepdg	Shepdg	Shepdg	Shepdg	Shepdg	Shepdg
Tinsley	Plough	Plough	Plough	Thrashing	Thrashing	Dung Ca
Harding	Joby	Joby	Spring Straw	Joby	Bockham	Dressing
Bowper	Harrow	Harrow	Harrow	Thrashing	Thrashing	Dung Co
Hait	Joby	Joby	Joby	Joby	Joby	Joby
Harding	Shepdg	Shepdg	Shepdg	Shepdg	Shepdg	Shepa
J. Hiler	Plough	Plough	Oakley St	Thrashing	Thrashing	Bedford
Curtis	Birds	Birds	Birds	Birds	Birds	Birds
Woods	Birds	+	+	+	+	+

The work register for West End Farm, Stevington, for 8–13 April 1889. The weekly wages (not shown) ranged from 2s 5d (12p) for Curtis and Woods, the bird scarers, to 14s 6d (72½p) for George and Robert Tysoe for threshing. The agricultural depression, caused by poor summers and the influx of cheap wheat from America, resulted in widespread hardship in the county from the 1880s. Wages increased only a little throughout the century and many labourers emigrated with their families.

A studio portrait of a Shillington farm labourer in the 1880s. He is wearing clothing typical of the nineteenth-century farm worker – a smock, long gaiters and heavy lace-up boots.

A farmer with a three-horse seeding team on Stockingstone Hill, Luton, looking towards Limbury and Biscot. Old Bedford Road is in the middle distance with North Lodge in the centre, and New Bedford Road is beyond. The picture was taken by Luton's earliest photographer James Davis in the 1890s. Below, a ploughing team is at work near Aspley Guise, *c.* 1900.

A three-horse reaper near Stopsley in the 1890s. Machinery gradually supplanted reaping by hand towards the end of the century. This is another picture by James Davis, who also worked as a harmonium maker and later as a straw hat manufacturer.

The Davey family of Prebendal Farm, Bedford, pause while binding wheat at Queen's Park. In the pony and trap Emily Davey holds her infant son Reginald; William Henry Davey is seated in the centre. The picture was taken by E. Walker and Co. of Bedford in about 1896.

Although these photographs were taken nearly forty years apart they show that little had changed in the threshing process during the first half of the twentieth century. Isaac Parker is standing next to his engine at College Farm, Great Barford, in about 1905 (above), and the same job is in progress near Northill in August 1939 (below). Combine harvesters have greatly reduced the labour involved in farming for they bring together the processes of cutting and threshing corn.

Willington farm labourers sharpen their scythes at haytime, *c.* 1900. By this time the traditional farm labourers' smock had largely disappeared, but their dress, with patterned handkerchiefs in evidence, is still distinctive. The labourers' dinner in the field was often the Bedfordshire 'clanger', a pasty with meat at one end and jam at the other.

Men building a haystack at Maulden in March 1941, captured by a *Bedfordshire Times* photographer. Fortunately for us the staff on the newspaper realized that traditional agricultural scenes were worth recording before they disappeared, and they took many local views from the late 1930s onwards.

Bert Purser fills up the grain bags after threshing at Queen's College Farm, Oakley, *c.* 1935. The Fowler traction engine which worked the threshing tackle was owned by Ralph Savage of Riseley and hired out to local farmers.

Gleaners near Lodge Farm, Riseley, *c.* 1900. Levi Webb of Willington, interviewed in 1939, recalled gleaning (picking up ears of corn left by the reapers) in his youth: 'An oldish man was told off every morning to ring the bell at 7 o'clock and again at 6 o'clock at night. Gleaners were not supposed to start before the bell. They would take dinner with them, probably cold potatoes.'

Steam-engine and binder belonging to T.B. Kitchener and Co. of Potton, *c.* 1910. This scene was recorded by George B. Symonds, a local photographer. Henry Kitchener, owner of the firm of agricultural machinists, stands by the binder.

Farm workers and steam-engine at Potton, *c.* 1920. George Clark, standing in front of the engine, worked for Kitchener's most of his life and died in 1954. When he worked at villages such as Willington, a few miles away, he would leave Potton at 3 a.m. to walk there and at night he would walk home again. Bert Albone stands on the left of the group, but the other two men are unidentified.

Henlow surveyors at work from the enclosure map of *c.* 1798. The replacement of the medieval system of strip farming by large enclosed fields occurred sporadically from the sixteenth century, but gathered pace in the period between 1794 and 1819 when the majority of enclosures by Act of Parliament occurred in the county. John Goodman

Maxwell of Spalding, appointed surveyor of the Henlow enclosure, painted this picture on the map of his men at work. The team are using surveying instruments while a countryman and his dog look on.

Weighing seed potatoes at Church Farm, Cockayne Hatley, *c.* 1910. The potatoes are being taken from the clamp at the back of the shed and riddled to remove the loose earth. Bad potatoes were removed at this stage and then the crop was put into sacks and weighed on the weighing machines in the foreground.

Harvesting potatoes at Great Barford in the late 1930s. The Oliver tractor, driven by Fred Southall, was the first of its type to be imported from the United States in 1937.

Carrot bunchers at the back of the Rose and Crown pub at Girtford, near Sandy, c. 1910. The men, who worked for John Barringer, a local market gardener, are, left to right: Sam Norman, Jacob Martin, Percy Peers, Jim Brown, Sid Page and an unidentified man.

Harvesting plums at Eaton Bray in the 1950s. The Aylesbury prune, a variety of cooking plum, was grown at Billington, Stanbridge, Totternhoe and Eaton Bray as well as in several Buckinghamshire villages near the foot of the Chiltern Hills. Foreign imports, rising labour costs, and the development of new varieties of plums killed off the trade by the early 1960s.

William Cherry shepherding sheep down Elstow High Street, *c.* 1900. He lived with his wife Eliza, a lace-maker, in Bunyan's cottage, Elstow, for more than sixty years. Their son Alfred was a professional cricketer who played for Bedfordshire.

Sheep shearing at Institute Farm, Ridgmont, *c.* 1900. The farm was part of the County Agricultural Education Institute which opened in January 1896 to provide training in a wide variety of subjects including dairy farming, horticulture and bee keeping. The institute closed in 1913 shortly after Frank Spooner, the director of education, embezzled the funds and fled to Madeira.

A farmer and his men prepare to coax sheep through the dip at Caddington in 1907. The current controversy over the alleged ill-effects of sheep-dip continues to rumble on, but no one gave it much thought at the turn of the century.

Brothers W. (left) and R. Stringer digging peat on Flitwick Moor in October 1948. Peat was dug here from at least the early seventeenth century, and between 1910 and 1967 was transported to Leicester, Nottingham, Desborough and other places where it was used to purify coal gas. The moor is now a home for wild plants.

Riseley woodmen pose with their tools in the early 1920s. The men are, left to right: William Wildman (or 'Bingy'), Alfred Bass, Walter Hancock, Joseph Hancock (or 'Tiny'), Arthur Wagstaffe, ? Hopkins, -?-, and Elijah Litchfield (carpenter and wheelwright).

A steam-engine running a saw at Town Farm, Riseley, *c.* 1910. The man leaning on the stick, second from the right, is probably David Waldock of Town Farm.

Pavenham men return from cutting the grass for strewing in the church, *c.* 1955. The traditional grass strewing took place annually on Feast Sunday, the first Sunday after 11 July, in honour of St Peter.

This wagon was owned by the Topham family who farmed at Honeydon, Eaton Socon. When this picture was taken in about 1900 countless horses and carts were used on the land, but with the arrival of the lorry and the tractor in ever-increasing numbers, they are now consigned to history.

Wet weather in June 1953 increased the danger of blight in potato crops. This helicopter, owned by Pest Control Ltd of Cambridge, is seen taking off to spray plants in the Wyboston area.

SECTION TWO

Manufacturing

Dan Albone (1860–1906), Biggleswade's most famous son, on his Ivel racing cycle, *c.* 1886. Dan was an indefatigable cyclist. By 1881 he had opened the Ivel Cycle Works in Biggleswade. In the early 1900s he developed the first motor tractor and a forerunner of the tank.

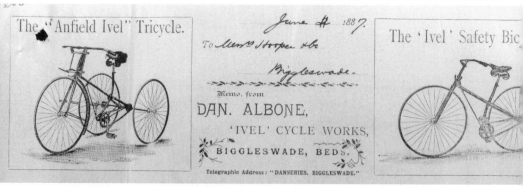

The "Anfield Ivel" Tricycle.

June 4 1887.

To Messrs Hooper & Co

Biggleswade.

Memo. from
DAN. ALBONE,
'IVEL' CYCLE WORKS,
BIGGLESWADE, BEDS.

Telegraphic Address: "DANNERIES, BIGGLESWADE."

The 'Ivel' Safety Bic

Dan Albone was an inventor and entrepreneur of great versatility. This billhead of 1887 shows two of his famous Ivel cycles.

A fire engine also designed by Dan Albone turns into Sun Street, Biggleswade, past the Royal Oak Inn, *c.* 1900. Dan was born at the nearby Ongley Arms, later called the Ivel Hotel. The firm did not long survive Dan's death, for it lost money during the First World War and went into receivership in 1920.

The inventor Herbert Percy Saunderson (1867–1939) founded Elstow Works near Cow Bridge, Kempston, in 1900, where he designed tractors, cars and aircraft until 1920. His petrol-driven car (above), shown here in 1896, was successful, although the inventor was fined at Wellingborough for driving without a man with a red flag in front. Another drawback was that as the engine was under the seats the passengers had to alight frequently to cool off. The tractor (below) drawing a plough in a field near the works was based on a lorry chassis. The photograph dates from about 1904.

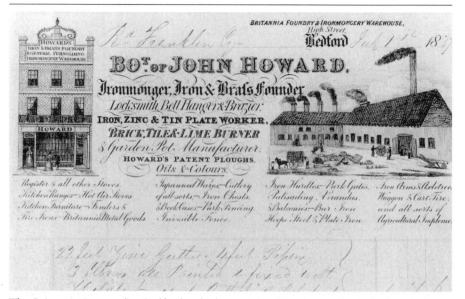

The Britannia Ironworks, Bedford, which specialized in the production of agricultural implements, was founded by John Howard (1791–1878) in 1813, and continued by his sons. The billhead of 1837 shows the new shop and works built on the site of the Barley Mow pub in the High Street. John Howard retired from the business in 1851 and his sons James and Frederick built the new works in Kempston Road between 1857 and 1859. The lower picture shows the smithery in the 1880s.

The Howards made a great contribution to the improvement of agricultural machinery and their works at Bedford attracted many visitors, including the Italian patriot Garibaldi in April 1864. A double-ended steam plough is being displayed in the yard in about 1870, and the Crown Inn in Britannia Road is in the background. The firm went into liquidation in 1932, seven years after the picture (below) of the fitting and erecting shop was taken. It later became part of the George Fischer group.

Brickyard workers at the New Road yard, Wilstead, operated by Charles Hebbes senior and his son between about 1885 and 1914. Several of the men are holding brick moulds. So closely did the mould become identified with the industry as a whole that representations of it were used in earlier times by some illiterate brickmakers as their mark on legal documents, instead of the usual cross.

A steam excavator at Wootton Pillinge brick works (called Stewartby after 1937) in the 1920s. In 1923 B.J. Forder and Sons Ltd amalgamated with the London Brick Company, with Halley Stewart as chairman. By the late 1930s the works at Stewartby, named after the chairman, were the largest in the world and employed 2,000 people to produce 500 million bricks annually.

Stewartby brick works in the 1930s. The chain-hauled wagons brought clay from the pits to the works.

Dunstable lime works was built *c.* 1903 on the Leighton Buzzard to Dunstable railway line and a few hundred yards from Dunstable North station. These pictures show operations in the early days of the works: men loading trucks with limestone at the

quarry face (top left), the incline tramway to the works (bottom left), the head of the incline (top right), and men loading limestone into railway wagons (bottom right).

Totternhoe lime kilns, 1912. Chalk was heated in the kilns and the resulting quicklime was used in agriculture to counteract acid soil. Limestone blocks were also used as building materials.

Sandwashing at Heath and Reach, *c.* 1910. The precise location of the quarry and the firm involved is unknown but it could be the Stone Lane Hill sand pit owned by Joseph Arnold of Leighton Buzzard. Leighton Buzzard and district is still famous for its high quality building sand which is exported as far afield as Saudi Arabia.

The pattern shop at Bagshawe and Co. Ltd, chain manufacturers of Dunstable, *c.* 1920. The pattern makers are, left to right: Adam McIntosh, Ernest Bliss, George Jackson and Fred Stearn. The firm, which was founded by Arthur Bagshawe (1859–1926), moved from London to Dunstable in 1906 and closed down in 1972.

The firm J. Harrison Carter, makers of agricultural machinery, was founded in Bullpond Lane, Dunstable, in 1894, and provided work for local people made unemployed by the decline of the straw-plait industry. The firm was taken over by Johansson in the 1930s and survived until the 1950s. This photograph shows the workshop in the 1920s.

Lathe operators and office clerks at George Kent Ltd of Luton, meter manufacturers, *c*. 1914. The firm originated in London in the 1830s and its main product was the rotary knife-cleaning machine until a patent for a water meter was purchased in 1883. Air, gas and steam meters were manufactured at the Luton works which opened in 1908.

A traction engine belonging to Ralph Savage of Riseley taking a tree trunk to Astells timber merchants in Ampthill Street, Bedford. The scene was captured by local photographer Donald Lindley outside his Tavistock Street shop on 20 July 1925. Aubrey Savage stands by the engine; his assistant is Jake Clark of Swineshead. Ralph Savage owned the first binder in Riseley as well as the second motor car in the village, a Ford Model T of 1928.

Rolls of wallpaper being delivered on Midland Railway carts to Frederick Gale's decorating and plumbing business at 3 Cardington Road, Bedford, c. 1902. In the days before heavy lorries, bulky manufactured goods could only be moved from railheads in a lumbering caravan of horse-drawn vehicles.

The workshops of Nicholls and Son, the Bedford motor engineers, *c.* 1920. In the upper picture (left to right) Sam Iliffe, Frank Claridge, foreman Fred Pilgrim and Ted Sparrow are at work in the body shop. Frank Hammond is vulcanizing tyres in the lower picture. The firm was started as a coachbuilders by William Henry Nicholls in the 1880s, acquired Deane and Son (Bedford Carriage Works) in 1911, and successfully adapted to car-body building. It closed in about 1970.

Two views of the Vauxhall Motors assembly line in 1935, showing the early stages of chassis assembly (above) and a Light Six on the brake adjustment machine before taking to the road for testing (below). The firm was founded in 1857 as an iron works at Vauxhall, London, and began manufacturing cars in 1903 before the move to Luton in 1905.

Joseph Hermann Homann's cardboard box factory and delivery vans in Havelock Road, Luton, *c.* 1910. Joseph Homann was probably a first or second generation immigrant from Germany. He married Elizabeth Yuill, a printer's daughter, at Luton in 1898 and died in 1941.

Employees of Samuel Wells (Biggleswade Brewery) pose for the camera in the 1890s. The firm was bought in 1898 by George Winch, a Chatham solicitor, for £144,000 and renamed Wells and Winch. The brewery was substantially rebuilt in 1903 and was eventually taken over by Greene King in 1961.

Samuel Hallum, Fred Pressland, Charles Leonard and Jack Usher are seen (left to right) in the Biggleswade Brewery maltings in 1912. In 1929 the building was converted into a bottling plant and in 1955 into a mineral factory.

A Charles Wells brewery lorry outside the Saracen's Head, Bedford, during the silver jubilee celebrations for King George V and Queen Mary in 1935. The brewery in Horne Lane was built between 1818 and 1836 and demolished in 1976, business being transferred to a newly built brewery in Havelock Street.

The carvers' shop at the Pyghtle works in the 1920s. The works, which specialized in architectural woodwork, were founded in 1896 and quickly achieved a high reputation, opening Bond Street showrooms in 1906. Despite a fire on 21 October 1924 the firm continued to expand and was commissioned to make some of the fittings for the Shakespeare Memorial Theatre at Stratford-upon-Avon in 1932. In June 1960 the firm merged with Samuel Elliott (Reading) Ltd of Caversham and the Bedford works were closed.

The foundry at W.H. Allen and Co. Ltd in 1916. This famous engineering firm was founded by William Henry Allen at Lambeth in 1880, moved to Bedford in 1893, and is now part of the Rolls Royce Industrial Power group. Allen's built steam engines and electric generators for the White Star liner *Titanic* which sank in 1912.

The crash of the R101 at Beauvais on 5 October 1930 marked the end of the project to build enormous passenger-carrying airships. This photograph shows the nose of the sister ship R100 being dismantled at Cardington on 3 December 1931.

Aircraft and caravans under construction in the workshops of the Berkeley Coachworks at Hitchin Street, Biggleswade, *c.* 1950. The firm became Berkeley Cars Ltd in 1956 and closed down in about 1960.

Packers at Meltis, the Bedford firm of confectionery manufacturers, in the 1960s. This scene has changed little since the firm was founded in 1913 by the Bermondsey-based company Peek Freans to make the Meltis chocolate confectionery range.

SECTION THREE

Who Will Buy . . . ?

Leighton Buzzard market by local photographer William F. Piggott, 1890s. The market still takes place on Tuesdays and Saturdays but it consists entirely of stalls; the livestock has disappeared. The market cross dates from the fifteenth century.

Bedford market on St Paul's Square, *c.* 1890. This was the traditional scene for many years until the market was moved to a less cramped site at Batts Ford in January 1986.

A busy scene at Stafford, Rogers and Merry cattle market in Horne Lane, Bedford, 1930s. The market was founded in 1865 and grew in importance when Irish store cattle were imported for sale there in 1929. It closed in the 1960s.

A busy parade of shops in Ford End Road, Bedford, *c*. 1910. No. 8 is Dudeney and Johnston Ltd, grocer's, then comes William Sanders' greengrocer's at No. 10 and William Welch's boot stores at No. 12. Many of the shopkeepers and their families lived in the upper storeys.

Mrs Naomi Lowe stands outside her post office and general stores in Flitton High Street in the 1930s. The shop is a makeshift construction of wooden boards and corrugated iron, but is brightened up by the tinplate advertisements.

Mrs Cree stands in the doorway of the general stores in Hitchin Road, Arlesey, in the 1930s. Then as now local stores were a focal point of village life, but shops like these are now under relentless pressure from rising costs and competition from supermarkets. The advertisement in the left-hand window, 'Boy Wanted Here', gives a reminder of an age without laws against sex discrimination in employment.

Joseph and Walter Baker's hardware shop at 14 Church Street, Dunstable, *c.* 1900. A great variety of goods are for sale including basins at 1*d* each and zinc buckets at 6½*d*.

Butchers at work. In the upper picture Jabez Thorne of Eaton Bray pauses by his cart in the act of sharpening his knife on a steel, *c.* 1910. W.H. Stooks (below) stands with his wife outside their shop on the corner of Park Road East and Gladstone Street, Bedford, in the early 1920s. As well as a fine display of meat they are showing off their prize certificates won at local shows. The three assistants on the left are, left to right: Mr Ward, Edward Fairey, who later worked for window cleaners 'Fairclean', and Ivy Stooks, later a hairdresser at Kempston. Of the group on the right only Ben Ward (in the centre), who later worked for Abbot's as a taxi-driver, is identified.

A MacFisheries wet fish van at Clophill, October 1920. The firm had a fishmonger's in Silver Street, Bedford, but also served local villages from its refrigerated van.

Bridgeman's fish shop in Iddesleigh Road, Queen's Park, Bedford, in the 1930s. As well as selling wet fish at prices which are a distant memory at between 6d and 11d per pound, fish was fried on request in the frier in the corner.

John White, wholesale fruiterer and banana merchant, at the wheel of his lorry outside his Midland Road stores in Bedford in the 1920s. Normally the bananas would be packed in boxes – so this display is probably for the photographer's benefit.

An unusual interior view of the Bedfordshire Autocar Co. Ltd showroom at 8–10 The Broadway, Bedford, in the mid-1920s. The firm was the authorized Ford dealer in Bedford but also sold farm machinery. In the distance St Peter's Green can be seen, while a man prepares to use the petrol pump which is operated by a hand-crank.

Two Bedfordshire garages in the 1920s. The Wilsons & Langley garage at 5–7 St Peter's Street, Bedford (above) traded at this address from about 1921 until 1934 when the site was cleared for the Granada Cinema, which was demolished in turn in 1991. Three lanes of traffic now roar past where the car is being filled up at the pump. Below is a view of Southam's garage at Bromham, then owned by Major Hill, *c.* 1920.

Two three-wheeled handcarts belonging to Biddenham Dairies in Grafton Road, Bedford, in the 1920s. The milk was poured from the churns into the bottles, unlike today when milk is delivered in sealed bottles.

A peaceful rural scene at Lidlington in the 1920s. The local milkman Mr Humphreys poses with his horse and cart at the start of his round.

Door-to-door deliveries by the baker are now history, although some milkmen still deliver bread. John Ray, the Langford baker, poses with his family, *c.* 1900. In the lower picture, Ken Richardson of Wilstead delivers bread to The Bell pub at Cotton End, Cardington, in the 1920s. Richardson's van has been fitted with pneumatic tyres to give a more comfortable ride, but apart from that little has changed in the quarter of a century between the two photographs.

A grocer's cart belonging to Jelley & Clarke of Bedford outside the shop belonging to Frederick William Littlechild, a fellow grocer at Sandy. The driver is well wrapped up against the weather, with an overall and two coats on.

William Welch's boot repairing depot at 2 Midland Road, Bedford, *c.* 1914, with rolls of leather and a fine display of period advertising outside. In 1914 William Welch also had shops in Ford End Road and St Cuthbert's Street, but by 1920 only the Midland Road shop survived.

FLITWICK.

A REMARKABLE
ENGLISH MEDICINAL SPRING

Which yields the most Valuable Specific yet discovered,

— FOR —

ANÆMIA (Poorness of Blood),
RHEUMATISM, INDIGESTION,
GENERAL DEBILITY,

AND IS THE ●————————————● AND NEURALGIA,

Most · Invigorating · Tonic
in the World.

THE HIGHEST AWARD
Was given by the following eminent Scientific Judges:—

THOMAS GREENISH, Esq.	Professor T. REDWOOD.
THOMAS HYDE HILLS, Esq.	E. BUCHANAN BAXTER, M.D.
PETER SQUIRE, Esq.	Dr. WINTER BLYTH.
Dr. ROBERT FARQUHARSON, M.P.	G. W. WIGNER, F.C.S.
W. MURRELL, Esq., M.D., F R.C.P. *(Lond.)*	

☞ THE ONLY CHALYBEATE WHICH HAS GAINED THE DISTINCTION. ☜

OPINIONS OF MEDICAL EXPERTS.

A M.A., M.D., WRITES : { "FLITWICK is an isolated production of Nature—
unrivalled, unimitated, inimitable."

A M.R.C.S. WRITES :—" In cases of Dyspepsia, Indigestion, Anæmia, or poorness of blood, and affections of the nerves, FLITWICK is simply invaluable."

A M.D., M.R.C.S., WRITES :—" FLITWICK is invaluable for backward children. For Neuralgia it renders the greatest possible service."

A Senior Physician to the Royal Chest Hospital WRITES :—" I do not hesitate to pronounce it the very best tonic the United Kingdom possesses."

A M.D., Surgeon to the late Duke of Albany, WRITES :—" FLITWICK possesses most valuable tonic properties."

A M.R.C.S. WRITES :—" FLITWICK Chalybeate is really an excellent tonic. I use it largely, and have found it most useful in all forms of Anæmia, and particularly Chlorosis."

A L.R.C.P., M.R.C.S., L.S.A., L.M., WRITES :—" FLITWICK is agreeable to take. It is especially suitable for ladies and children, and can be prescribed where other forms of iron would be inadmissible."

A M.D., M.R.C.S., WRITES :—" It would be impossible to speak too highly in commendation of FLITWICK."

☞ "LANCET" REPORT ON FLITWICK. ☜
OCTOBER 24th, 1891.

" *Far superior to artificial compounds.*"
" *A most valuable form of iron in remarkable quantity.*"
" *Eminently fitted for speedy absorption and assimilation into the system.*"
" *Agreeably acid to the taste, and most palatable with good lemonade.*"

SOLD IN BOTTLES, 1/6 AND 2/6 EACH, OF ALL CHEMISTS.

Wholesale Depôt : 63, BOROUGH HIGH STREET. S.E.

Advertisement for waters from the Flitwick Spring, *c.* 1900. The so-called spring was in fact a fraud. Henry King Stevens pumped ordinary water twice through bags of peat on the moor to produce a sherry-coloured liquid strongly impregnated with minerals. The waters were sold until about 1930.

Craftsmen at work. John King, saddler and harness maker, is shown in his workshop at 42 Tavistock Street, Bedford, *c.* 1900. The family ran a shop in Bedford from the 1870s until the mid-1930s. Francis Osborn (1846–1941) was a watchmaker at 24 Harpur Street, Bedford, from 1870 until his death. He is shown in his workshop in the late 1930s holding part of the framework of a skeleton clock.

SECTION FOUR

At Your Service

In this rare photograph the travelling photographer William Micklethwaite stands outside his studio, probably at Biggleswade in the early 1870s. Micklethwaite launched his business in Newry, Co. Down, Ireland, in the 1850s, came to England for a few years, and then emigrated to Canada in the 1870s. Travelling photographers were sometimes resented in larger towns with established firms of photographers.

The servants at Bushmead Priory, Eaton Socon, pose for the camera, *c.* 1900. They are, left to right: Charlie Childs, coachman; Kate Caress, cook; Bert Ruff, jun., gardener's boy, who later owned a garage at Little Staughton and died in 1964; Madge(?) Wade-Gery, the daughter of the house, aged six; Daisy Ball, parlourmaid; Annie Green, housemaid and dairymaid; and Bert Ruff, gardener.

Sharnbrook gamekeeper Thomas Glover Pacey (1841–97) poses with his dog and gun in the 1880s. He started off life as an agricultural labourer but was a gamekeeper by 1871. His son Thomas Harry Pacey was a builder at Sharnbrook.

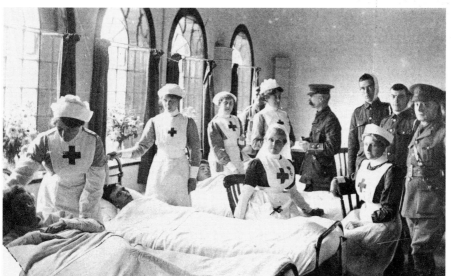

Nurses, soldiers and patients in a ward at Leighton Buzzard workhouse, Grovebury Road, during the First World War. Nurse Eileen is seated and marked with a cross. During the war workhouses and local houses such as Woburn Abbey, Wrest Park and Hinwick House provided accommodation in auxiliary hospitals for casualties sent from the front.

The Bedford, Harrold and Wellingborough carrier's van in the 1880s, photographed at an unknown location. Unlike the stagecoach, carriers generally survived the arrival of the railways and some lasted until after 1900.

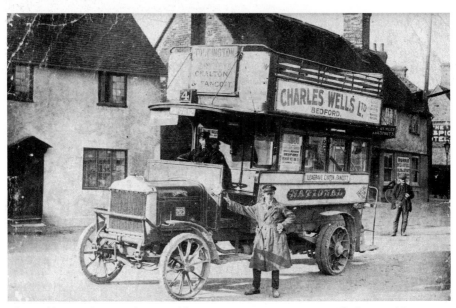

The Toddington bus ran from Toddington to Luton via Fancott, Chalton and Leagrave. Here the driver and conductor pose with their bus near The Bell, Toddington, in the early 1920s.

Ouse Transport Company steam launch and barge on the River Ouse, possibly near Bedford, *c.* 1895. The river navigation was important for coal and other traffic from King's Lynn in the seventeenth and eighteenth centuries but was eventually shut down in 1876–8 after years of neglect and railway competition. It was briefly revived between 1893 and 1897 when Leonard Simpson formed the Ouse Transport Company.

The Grand Union canal passes near the south-west county boundary at Leighton Buzzard and Linslade. A loaded barge belonging to the carriers Harvey Taylor of Aylesbury unloads at the wharf belonging to Brantoms, the Leighton Buzzard millers, seedsmen and forage merchants, in the 1920s. The channel is now filled in and the wharf buildings demolished, but the footbridge survives.

The staff of R.V. Dove's, window cleaners, pose outside their depot at 24 Queen Street, Bedford, in the 1930s. The staff are, left to right: Sammy Nutt, -?-, -?-, -?-, Chick Chester, Ernie Flanders, -?-, Fred Ball, Bert Knight, Horace Rootham, Gordon Dove, -?-, Ernest Carpenter, Fred Brittain, Alf Raspberry (who was killed at the fall of Singapore in 1942), Ted Pilgrim, J.W. Riley, R.V. Dove. In the early 1930s the firm cleaned 146 windows at the County (now South Wing) Hospital for £2 10s 5d (£2.52).

The draymen at Wells & Winch, formerly Biggleswade Brewery, in 1913. The men are, back row, left to right: Charles Daniels, John Green, Alf Albone, Mr Matthews, Fred Brown, Albert Clark. Middle row: Sid Payne, Bill Walker, Charlie Kitchener, Jim Sells, Amos Wells. Lying on the ground are Jack Usher and A. Lincoln.

A working party clearing the banks of weeds on the Ivel at Biggleswade, *c.* 1910. This is just another example of a labour-intensive job now made easier by modern equipment such as the strimmer.

A roadman working on a lonely stretch of highway leading towards the Knoll, Totternhoe. The photograph was taken by Arthur Anderson of Luton in 1903 and was subsequently published as a postcard.

Workmen widening the road at Puddle Hill, Houghton Regis, in the early 1930s. This was part of the A5 improvement scheme which took five years and cost over £270,000. The chalk and gravel is being removed by hand before being loaded on to the tipper trucks on the plateway.

Maintaining the roads is one of the never-ending tasks carried out by local authorities and their workforce. Above, workmen are grouped around a horse-drawn tar boiler in Dunstable in the 1920s. Once their job was done the asphalt would be rolled by a steamroller as in the 1911 picture below of the Highways Department roller belonging to Bedfordshire County Council. The men, left to right, standing, are: Tom Wagstaff, Mr Hullatt of Eaton Socon, -?-, Mr Partridge of Bletsoe, -?-. F. Payne is the flagman on the roller. The last Bedfordshire County Council steamroller was sold in 1961.

Building up and breaking down. In the upper picture workmen engaged on the restoration of Elstow parish church in 1880–2 pose for the camera by the north door. The old church was considered so dangerous that large portions were rebuilt, including the south aisle and parts of the nave and clerestory. In the lower picture men are busy demolishing a pillbox at Shefford in September 1945, one of the many obsolete defences taken down after the Second World War.

Sightseers watch the main sewer being dug in Shortmead Street, Biggleswade, 1908. The palisades are being used to shore up the sides of the hole while the warning flag is for the benefit of passers-by. This view, taken by local photographer Henry Drysdale, is looking north from the Sun Street junction. The wall surrounding the Ivel Bury estate is in the background on the right.

Laying the water mains at Sandy, *c.* 1905. This is another view by Henry Drysdale, the Biggleswade photographer.

Workmen laying gas mains near St Cuthbert's Church, Bedford, on 3 December 1900 (above), and in Bedford Road, Kempston, in June 1925 (below). The second view, with the generator and pneumatic drill, would not be out of place today, except that such work no longer attracts crowds of onlookers.

George Bartle was a market gardener and builder at Potton. Here his men are at work on Bury Hill bridge, Potton, which was completed in 1894. Among the onlookers is postman Mr Winters with his bicycle.

In 1906 part of the old Harpur Trust Hospital (children's home) was gutted to build a new gymnasium for Bedford Modern School. The gym became the school hall in the 1920s and the whole site was cleared for a shopping centre when the school moved from Harpur Street to Manton Lane in 1974. Boots the Chemists is now on the site shown in the photograph, but the façade of the school (not shown) and tower designed by Edward Blore still stand.

In 1902 a new 180 ft well was sunk near New Spring Farm to supply water for Biggleswade and district. The first of these two views, taken in December 1902, shows a workman in the gloom at the bottom of the well without any protective clothing or a hard hat. The greensand and clay was loaded by hand into buckets and drawn up by the steam crane. The well was fitted with pumping machinery to serve a reservoir built in 1904 at Topler's Hill about a mile away.

BEDFORD SANITARY LAUNDRY.

WORKS:

SANDHURST ROAD.
AMPTHILL ROAD,

Manageress:—
Miss BELL.

Registered Offices:—

1, St. PAUL'S SQUARE.
BEDFORD.

Secretary.—
G. C. WALKER,
AUCTIONEER &
ESTATE AGENT.

A LAUNDRY for Private Family Washing, with every Hygienic Provision and the most Approved Appliances.

The whole of the Sanitary Arrangements are under the supervision of the Bedfordshire Sanitary Association.

ILLUSTRATED GUIDE & PRICE LIST
forwarded on application.

XLV

In the days before the household washing machine and the launderette, the local laundry was big business. The Bedford Sanitary Laundry, shown in an advertisement of 1906, had receiving and sorting rooms, washing rooms, and ironing, airing and packing rooms. The laundry was delivered by horse-drawn vans, such as the Haddon Sanitary Laundry van below, until they were superseded by motor vans in the 1920s. The Haddon Sanitary Laundry ceased trading by 1920, but Bedford Sanitary Laundry lasted until about 1967.

Two views of Bedfordshire smithies in about 1900 when work was plentiful, thanks to the thousands of horses used in agriculture and transport. In the upper picture Frederick George Crouch (1863–1941) stands in the doorway of Harrold smithy where he worked for sixty-five years. His workman Alfred Robinson is on the left. Apart from their work shoeing horses it is clear that bicycles and farm machinery were also repaired. In the lower picture Turvey blacksmiths are shoeing a horse.

The village blacksmith was a virtually extinct breed when John Ryan of Clophill was photographed at his forge in August 1963. He was one of about two dozen 'readjusted' blacksmiths in the country who passed an examination on diseases of horses' feet and other topics, so ensuring his survival in a changing world.

William Kendall's wheelwright's yard at Wilstead, *c.* 1908. The people are, left to right: Ellen and Thomas Kendall, Mrs Elizabeth Kendall, Florence Kendall, employee 'Jocka' Britten, William Kendall (at the saw bench).

Newland & Nash dairymen's cart at the Crown Inn, Bromham, *c.* 1895. James Rust was the licensee and his wife stands in the doorway. The inn was demolished in 1905 when Bromham bridge was widened.

The power of the press. The compositors' rooms at Spong and Son, printers, of Biggleswade (above), *c*. 1914, and at the Mill Street offices of the *Bedfordshire Times* at Bedford in the 1920s (below). The overseer, George Loveday, is on the extreme left. The printing blocks were made and set up in these rooms, a very slow and laborious process. The *Bedfordshire Times*, established in 1845, used this method until 'photo-composite', involving the use of bromide prints, was developed in *c*. 1969. This was superseded in 1990 by the development of desk-top publishing.

A class at Queen's Park School, Bedford, *c.* 1905. The school log-books reveal the reality of teaching at this time, for as well as organizing work and examinations the staff had to cope with outbreaks of scarlet fever and other diseases. Several children admitted were 'poorly nourished and backward'. The school was opened by the Duke of Bedford on 8 April 1899.

Children examining and watering plants in the conservatory of Bedford Kindergarten College and Preparatory School in 1901. This picture is in great contrast to the usual school pictures of this date, with children behind ranks of desks.

Two views of the Bedford Professional String Band, which flourished from 1893 to 1916, both from *c*. 1900. In the upper picture the bandsmen are, left to right: J. Tucker (cornet), F. Ellison (clarinet), G. Brown (violinist, leader), Charlie Voice (harpist), G. Welling (bass). Mr Tucker, a humorous and persuasive Irishman, went round with the hat. The Swan Hotel gardens (below) was a popular venue.

Gone for a soldier. These pictures, by Bedford photographer Henry Kingham, show Bedfordshire Regiment recruits on joining at Kempston barracks in 1894 and again at camp after three months training. Even apart from the prospect of disease or death in the field army life was harsh. Albert Culpin of Shillington, who enlisted in 1877, wrote to his family: 'I will tell you a bit about food and bed; breakfast, bread and coffee; dinner, meat and potatoes; tea, bread and tea; straw bed and pillow, 2 blankets and 2 sheets – it makes me think about your good beds.'

The 2nd battalion, Bedfordshire Regiment, was raised in Ireland in 1858, and served continuously on garrison duty in India between 1876 and 1899. In this picture soldiers are posing with machine-guns at the School of Musketry at Secunderabad in 1889.

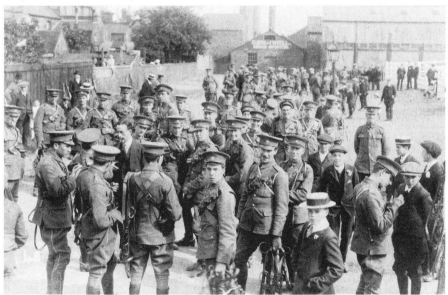

The Bedfordshire Yeomanry waiting for their horses to be unboxed near the cattle pens at Bedford Midland Road goods station, c. 1915. The backs of houses in Prebend Street are on the left, with the Elders and Fyffes banana warehouse in the background. The Bedfordshire Yeomanry served on the Western Front in the First World War and lost only forty-three men against over six thousand in the Bedfordshire Regiment.

Mail being collected from the *Graf Zeppelin* at Cardington in the 1930s by postmen Ralph Farmer (left) and Bill Rogers. The disaster involving the German airship *Hindenburg* at Lakehurst, USA, on 5 May 1937, also sounded the death knell for the *Graf Zeppelin*, and the end of an unusual postal service.

Postman William Southam giving a letter to Jane Harding at 4 High Street, Elstow, *c.* 1905. William Southam (1831–1908) was Elstow's sub-postmaster from 1871 and died in harness. His weekly wages over the period rose from 14*s* 8*d* (73p) to 16*s* 2*d* (81p). The Southams ran the post office as a family affair for years on end. William Southam's father, William senior, was in charge between 1859 and 1871 at £11 a year, while William junior was succeeded by his daughter Lily from 1908 to 1911 and his son Walter from 1911 until the late 1930s.

Postmen are still with us but the telegram and telegraph boy is only a memory, thanks to the telephone and the fax machine. Bedford telegraph boy E.W. Dockrill poses with his bicycle in 1921.

Shefford Fire Brigade outside the fire station built in Bridge Street to commemorate Queen Victoria's diamond jubilee in 1897. The station was opened on 11 May 1899 and this photograph was probably taken soon after. The man standing second from the right is Charles Johnson, who served from 1880 until 1915.

Kempston Fire Brigade pose with their rolled-up hoses, *c.* 1910. Until the 1930s fire brigades were composed of volunteers and relied on subscriptions for uniforms, engines and buildings. The Kempston Brigade, formed in 1907, was finally taken over by Kempston Urban District Council on 3 July 1934, but only after the firemen had threatened to resign.

Bedford Volunteer Fire Brigade practising pump drill at Longholme Lakes in the 1890s.

Longhurst & Skinner, COMPLETE HOUSE FURNISHERS, Midland Road, BEDFORD.

The BEDFORD PANTECHNICON, BEDFORD.

LONGHURST & SKINNER'S Premises shown in the above view are undoubtedly one of the most imposing buildings in the Furnishing Trade out of London and form a notable attraction to visitors to Bedford. It is necessary to pay a visit of inspection to these premises to realise the vast extent of their numerous showrooms. So varied is the stock that it is possible to absolutely purchase every household requisite to completely furnish any size residence without leaving **LONGHURST & SKINNER'S** premises.

XVII.

The Bedford Pantechnicon was a furniture warehouse built on the River Street and Midland Road corner in 1878. At about 3 a.m. on 11 January 1912 a fire broke out in the rug department on the first floor and, fanned by a stiff wind, the building burned to the ground. Four firemen received burns and Brigadier Burton was unconscious from the smoke for a time. The lower picture shows damping down in progress later that morning.

The funeral cortège of Captain Augustus Hill, Chief Officer of Bedford Volunteer Fire Brigade, passes along Midland Road towards St Paul's Church on 22 March 1912. Captain Hill was burned at the Pantechnicon fire – the ruins of which can be seen top left – but his injuries had healed and he died of long-standing neuritis. He was the last active original member of the brigade formed in 1870.

The projectionist at the Granada Cinema in Bedford prepares for a stage show starring Helen Shapiro, 6 February 1963. The Beatles, comparatively unknown at this stage in their careers, received only second billing. The Granada in St Peter's Street opened in 1934 and was demolished in 1991.

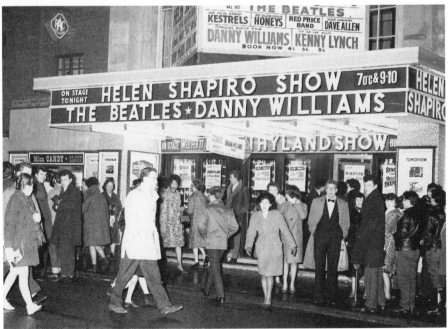

SECTION FIVE
Cottage Industry

Bedfordshire has a strong lace-making tradition, and while its origins are disputed, the legend that Katherine of Aragon taught her favourite art to people around Ampthill in the 1530s can be discounted. Rachel Read of Cranfield issued this trade card around 1900. She had customers as far afield as Manchester, Leeds, London and the United States.

Lace-makers at work in front of the kitchen range at Ridgmont post office, *c.* 1910. Mrs Hartwell (left) is winding bobbins while Mrs Sharpe, mother of the photographer Jack Sharpe, is working at her lace pillow. The spherical reflector on Mrs Sharpe's left directs the candlelight on to the pillow.

A Bedfordshire lace school, *c.* 1905. Specialist lace schools were established from the 1790s onwards and came into conflict with the system of compulsory general education introduced in the 1870s, especially as there was pressure from parents in poor families for their offspring to start earning as soon as possible.

Pavenham osier peelers at work, *c.* 1905. They are, left to right: Albert Smith, Polly Church, Lilian Wesley, Edie Huckle, Carrie Billing. Once the willows were dried, women stripped them of their skins with the aid of wooden sticks on which were fixed shaped bars of iron through which the willow rods were drawn to remove the bark. They were usually paid 3*d* (1½p) a bundle.

George Thornton, a Pavenham basket-maker, at work in 1907. Once the osiers had been peeled they were boiled, a process which dyed them, and after drying the basketwork could begin. Mr Thornton made his last basket at the age of eighty, in 1930, three years before his death.

Baskets were in great demand from farmers, market gardeners, post offices and laundries. Here the farmer at Hales Farm, Clifton, prepares to go to market with his family in about 1910. Occasionally orders for basketwork were more unusual – Miss Tucker of Pavenham Bury received a basketwork indoor kennel for her pet poodle as a wedding present in 1878.

Frederick Wells, basket-maker and market gardener, standing outside his shop and works in Hitchin Street, Biggleswade, c. 1914. The firm, founded by James Wells in 1830, managed about 100 acres of willows at its height, and ceased trading in 1936.

Mat-making was a particularly important industry in Pavenham. Every summer parties of men cut rushes on the Ouse or Nene, often taking tents with them so they could work for several days. Here George Jarvis and George Simcoe of Roxton are cutting rushes near their village, *c.* 1905.

Stacking the rushes to dry at Great Barford in 1939. By this time the local mat-making industry was in terminal decline: the last two makers, Harry Parrott of Bedford and George Purser of Pavenham, are listed in the 1936 *Kelly's Directory*, but had gone by 1940.

George Purser of Pavenham, probably the very last Bedfordshire mat-maker, at work in the 1920s. Rushes were made into hassocks, horse collars, baskets and matting for churches and the corridors of large buildings. George is plaiting at a long beam and the final 40 yd roll of matting could take a week to make. The industry died when cheap, prison-made, matting was imported from Holland and Belgium.

Charlotte Norris (*c.* 1816–1906) straw-plaiting in her cottage at Woodside, Caddington, *c.* 1890. She was the village midwife and also worked for the Crawley family at Stockwood House. Straw-plaiting was in decline when this picture was taken and the cottage industry was superseded by large hat factories.

Thatching has declined in Bedfordshire but there are still a few firms in the county. In this picture Mr G.R. Purser of Westoning, in the business for forty-four years, is thatching a cottage at Biddenham in April 1949.

Walter Parrott and his son Philip thatching at Pavenham, *c.* 1958. Walter is using an eave knife to trim the thatch while Philip holds the hazel sticks which are pinned down to hold the thatch in place. The introduction of modern machinery to replace the threshing box meant a shortage of long straw for the thatcher.

SECTION SIX

A Woman's Work . . .

This advertisement photograph, probably taken at Kempston in 1899, is obviously staged, but still gives an idea of the role of washerwoman and mother expected of most women at this period. The picture was taken by amateur photographer Alfred Burns (c. 1869–1936), bursar and secretary of Bedford Modern School for forty years.

School meals being served at Sharnbrook school in the 1930s. Meals were first provided on an experimental basis on 23 March 1925 and the service is thought to have been the first in the country. The dinner assistant on the left is probably Miss L. Bowler.

Mary Ball of Long Row, Pavenham, washing up at her stone sink in 1896. Conditions in many nineteenth-century cottages were primitive, as they were without mains drainage, gas or electricity.

The kitchen staff at Bedford County Hospital (now Bedford General Hospital, South Wing) shortly after it opened on 21 June 1899. Women comprised the majority of the nursing and domestic staff, but they were not admitted to the Board of Management until 1907.

The ironing department of Bedford Sanitary Laundry, Sandhurst Road, c. 1910. The department had '. . . a complete installation of Gas-heated Irons, the Heating of which can be regulated as required', but conditions must still have been arduous for the women who worked there.

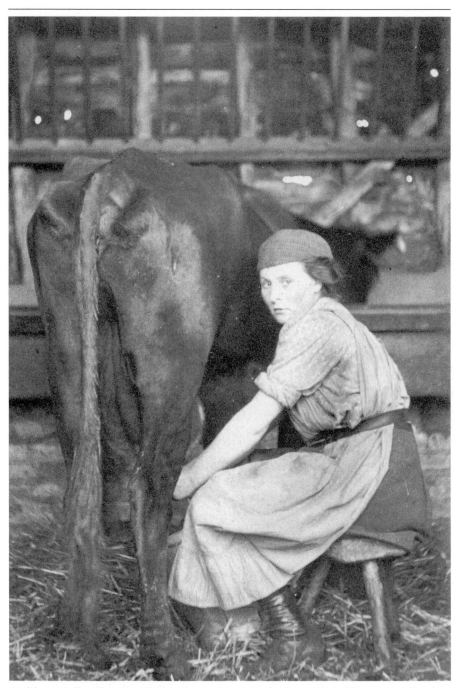

Kathleen Hull milking at Bridge Farm, Great Barford, *c.* 1914. These were the days before the electric milking machine and regulations on pasteurization and milk quotas.

Studio portrait of female workers at the Royal Airship Works run by Short Brothers at Cardington, *c.* 1918. They are both wearing triangular badges to show that they are on war service.

Women paring down gold-beater's skins to make airship fabric at Short Brothers, Cardington, *c.* 1918. Several layers of glue were added, and the fabric was stuck on the outer envelope of the airships. Conditions were probably better here than in the munitions factories, where chemicals dyed workers' skin yellow, earning women the nickname 'canary girls'.

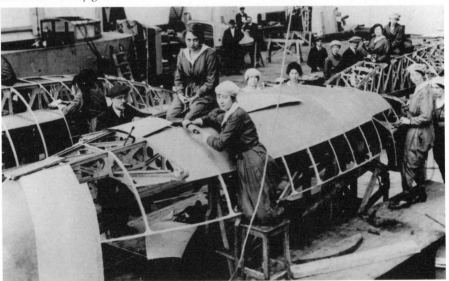

Workers fixing panels to airship R38 under construction at Cardington, *c.* 1920. The R38 made her maiden flight on 23 June 1921, but despite efforts to solve technical problems broke in two over the River Humber with heavy loss of life on 23 August.

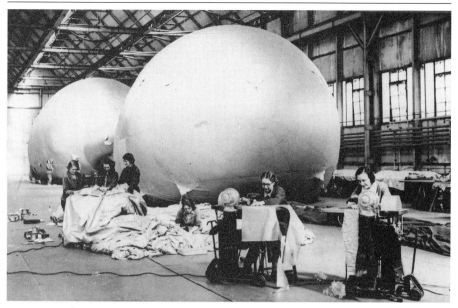

Women machining barrage balloon fabric at the Cardington airship sheds in the late 1930s. After the R101 disaster the Cardington sheds were little used, but in 1936 the site became RAF Cardington and between 1939 and 1948 was the headquarters of Balloon Command.

A wartime potato queue consisting mostly of women and children at Kingsbury Farm, Church Street, Dunstable, 7 April 1917. A note on the back of this picture, taken by local photographer James Field, reads: 'The potatoes were sold by Mr Gray at 1¾d per lb & only 2lb & sometimes 4lb were allowed at a time to one family.'

Women from agricultural college hoeing at Arlesey House, *c.* 1917. Unrestricted submarine warfare by Germany prompted the government to introduce the Cultivation of Lands Order in 1917. The policy was carried out by the War Agricultural Committee of Bedfordshire County Council and thousands of acres of pasture were ploughed up and seeded. Much of the work was done by women and prisoners of war.

Land Army girl Cathy Partridge with a haycart at Town Farm, Riseley, during the First World War.

Inflation, the pressures of war work, and the loss of skilled manpower caused labour problems during the First World War. This group shows women strikers at Luton, but it is unclear whether they worked at the Chaul End Munition factory, where the workers came out in May 1916, or at Vauxhall, which suffered a strike in February 1917.

Mary Quenby working at Bromham Mill, probably *c.* 1918. Bromham Mill was run by the Quenby family between 1905 and 1970, and Mary was in charge, earning £2 a week, after her father Harry and uncle Walter left the firm to go into farming.

Women roadsweepers in Mill Street, Bedford, 1916. The introduction of general conscription in 1916, after massive losses during the Battle of the Somme on the Western Front, meant the country depended more than ever on female labour.

Bedford postwomen in 1921. Women worked as clerical and counter staff in the nineteenth century but it was only during the First World War that they carried out postal (though not telegram) deliveries. They wore serge tunics and skirts, thick overcoats with red piping, and broad-brimmed hats.

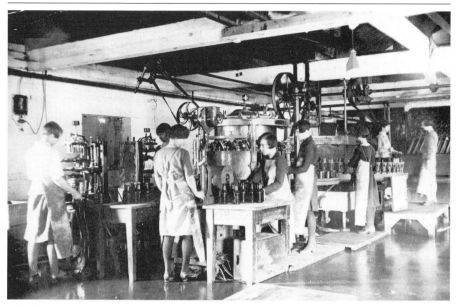

The bottling plant at Wells and Winch's Biggleswade Brewery, 1930. The women, left to right, are: Jess Champkins, Cis Fields, Elsie Beck, Gwen Faulkner, Betty Finding, Joyce Newman, May Boness.

Another war – another labour shortage. Twelve women porters, some of them evacuees from London, started work at Bedford Midland railway station in March 1941. Mrs Green told a reporter: 'We handle the mail-bags, fish boxes and the baggage. We are going to have uniforms shortly, and we have suggested slacks instead of skirts.'

Women engine cleaners at work at Bedford Midland sheds in May 1941. Six women started work in the locomotive department in April; the first was eighteen-year-old Mary Appleby of Bedford, formerly an usherette at an RAF camp cinema. The hours were 7.55 a.m. to 5.40 p.m., with an hour for lunch, and workers finished at midday on Saturday.

Beatrice Gooch, a former ambulance driver, was Bedford's first woman bus driver in October 1941. She was the first of five candidates to pass out of the Eastern National Company's new school for women drivers. Women with previous experience in driving heavy vehicles were required to replace men who had been called up.

During the Second World War W.H. Allen of Bedford employed women on a wide range of operations in the manufacture of electric motors and control gear for marine machinery. In this photograph, taken in April 1942, discs are being assembled on the armature hub of a 300 kw electric generator.

Women at work at London Brick's Stewartby works in the late 1940s. The workers are taking the 'green' clay bricks out of the presses and stacking them before they are sent to the kilns for firing.

SECTION SEVEN

Odd Jobs
and Time Off

'Leicester's unemployed march to London representing 2,000 men and their families', reads the banner. This picture shows the marchers passing through Dunstable in June 1905 with a brass band at their head. A few policemen are trying to keep back crowds of spectators.

James Clare of Woburn, imprisoned thirty-one times for poaching, was famous enough to inspire an engraving after his death. The original caption reads: 'On October last [1833] he was committed for ill-treating the mistress of Woburn Workhouse; and, agreeable to his many wishes, he died in Prison, in the 78th year of his age'. Offences against the rigorously enforced game laws were common in an age when rural poverty and unemployment were endemic.

Toddington gamekeeper Norman Snoxell (*c.* 1783–1855) poses with a poacher who is carrying a rabbit. This picture is thought to have been taken by William Cooper-Cooper of Toddington Manor in about 1854 and is one of the earliest known Bedfordshire photographs.

Travelling dealers and entertainers were common in Bedfordshire years ago. This cartoon of itinerant dealers in Dunstable ware was drawn by Woodward and Cruckshank and published in 1796. The crone and her younger companion are accompanied by a fierce dog.

Mr Gotzheim, an organ grinder who often visited Leighton Buzzard, c. 1910. Under the provisions of the Pedlars' Act (1871) the police granted certificates to wandering dealers and entertainers.

Isaac Parker of Great Barford demonstrates his potato knife-grinding machine, a wonderful Heath-Robinson contraption. Mr Parker also made a bird-scaring apparatus with four fearsome revolving metal cats and was well known as a fisherman and charmer of warts. The photograph was taken by Kingham of Bedford in about 1906.

Mr Blonden, the odd-job man, pauses for a smoke and a jug of ale in Mr Adam's garden at Ridgmont, c. 1900.

One of Toddington's church bells has just been unloaded from a lorry and is being slid along planks towards the hoist which will raise it up to the tower for rehanging. The Toddington bells were recast in 1906 by the Whitechapel bellfounders Mears and Stainbank.

The weathercock of St Paul's Church, Bedford, was repaired by the local ironmonger's, Henry Bacchus Ltd, and John Sayer is shown here refixing it on 2 April 1914. The engravings on the weathercock mention previous repairs and refixings back to 1867; the bullet hole was caused by a John York who fired a musket at it in about 1820.

These two views show a gas main being laid under the river between Queen's Park and Kempston on 8 March 1902. The portable generator pumped air into the diver's suit, which was very heavy and included lead-lined boots. The directors of Bedford Gas Company were not completely happy with the work carried out by the contractors, Aird and Co., for some of the joints in the main leaked and the work cost nearly double the estimate of £500.

An unusual way of cutting the grass. This lawnmower drawn by a donkey is in action at Toddington Manor in about 1900.

The staff of George Rushbrooke, an Ampthill draper and outfitter, practise their fire drill in the early years of this century. The picture was taken by local photographer John H. Copperwheat.

In the nineteenth century workers' clubs and social activities were gradually recognized as important ways of improving staff morale and productivity, as well as being enjoyable for all concerned. In the upper picture the employees at W.H. Allen, the Bedford engineering firm, are about to set off on a cycle ride. Work on the new factory, known as the Queen's Engineering Works, is not quite complete, which dates the picture to 1893–4. In the 1920s workers' outings by bus or charabanc, as shown below, became increasingly popular.

Occasional visits by royalty, politicians or other VIPs remain a feature of working life today, but gained extra significance in boosting morale and encouraging the war effort in the two world wars. King George V and Queen Mary visited the engineering works of W.H. Allen, Son and Co. Ltd, during a visit to Bedford on 27 June 1918. In this picture William H. Allen, the founder and chairman, is escorting the royal party from the offices.

The annual dinner or Christmas party is another way for workers to relax. The past and present pupil apprentices of W.H. Allen, Son and Co. Ltd of Bedford settle down for their fourth annual dinner at the Trocadero Restaurant in London, 22 October 1910.

A gentleman of the road. William Cunningham, also known as 'Old Henry', was a familiar sight in north Bedfordshire for more than a quarter of a century. Here he is by the roadside in the 1930s. When the photographer gave him two shillings he remarked: 'That won't buy much bitter!' For years he lived in a chicken house at Stagsden, before moving to a hut at Elstow. 'Old Henry' was found in a state of collapse by the roadside in January 1957 and died in hospital soon afterwards.

Name. *George Henry Charles Per...*

Description.

Age	32 years
Height	5/5
Hair	Dark
Eyes	Hazel
Complexion	Pale
Visage	Oval
Weight	152 lbs.
Trade	Clerk in orders
Where born	Guildford, Surrey
Last residence	Caldecot, Beds
Married or Single	Married
Religion	Ch: of Eng:
Read and Write	Well

This man is not what he seems! Despite his clothing and clerical 'dog-collar' George Perry was an accomplished fraudster and bigamist. He was committed to Bedford prison in December 1865 after his arrest for forging testimonials in order to become curate of Northill. Particularly notorious or persistent offenders were photographed under a shrewd policy instituted by the Governor of Bedford Prison, Robert Evan Roberts, in 1859. Perry's photograph was circulated to other police forces and a pattern of similar frauds emerged all over the country. At his trial in March 1866, where he received eighteen months' imprisonment, the court was packed with fashionable society.

Uncongenial employment. At Bedford gaol, pictured above in 1941, the inmates were set to work beating hemp as well as undergoing hard labour at shot drill and on the corn treadmill. Robert Evan Roberts, governor from 1853 to 1885, greatly expanded the industrial work of the prison, and mat-making and spinning were soon introduced. The receipt shows that a Mr Shepherd paid £5 5s 6d for two brush mats ordered in August 1865. The overall profit on prison labour was more than £18,000 in the period from 1853 to 1878, and Roberts also noted a reduction in breaches of prison rules under the new system.

Perils at work – Sharnbrook railway accident. A commemorative postcard sold to raise funds for the relatives of driver Arthur Coope and fireman John William Hawley who were killed when their express goods train from Manchester to London crashed into a fast goods train standing in Sharnbrook station at about 4 a.m. on 4 February 1909. The engine crew were burned in the wreckage, their bodies not being recovered until thirteen hours afterwards. The accident was caused by signalman Alfred Robins who pulled the wrong signal lever, so diverting the fast goods into the path of the express train. The photographs were taken by S. Percival of Kettering, and show the wholesale destruction of the wooden-bodied goods wagons.

Perils at work – Broom bridge disaster. The cast-iron bridge at Broom, built in 1823, was not designed to take the weight of heavy traction engines, and collapsed on 11 February 1873 under the weight of an engine owned by T.B. Kitchener of Potton. Of the men on the engine Walter Bonas of Biggleswade died of shock and exposure while a doctor was preparing to amputate his leg, and David Larman sustained serious head injuries.

ABNER COLSON,

(For 18 years Schoolmaster at Sharnbrook),

Born, 21st Nov., 1862.
Died, 10th Aug., 1908.

An acrostic

A friend sincere, to all his scholars dear :
B eloved by all, of him, they had no fear.
N one knew his worth, until Death's Angel came,
E nticing his spirit away from its earthly frame—
R ewarding his faithful service with " an honour'd name."

C ourage and zeal were in his genial nature seen,
O n every hand he helped, raised hopes where doubts had been.
L over of Music, his soul was all aflame ;
S unny his smile, to all he was the same.
O n his " good work " a monument in our memories we'll raise,
" N one knew him but to trust him, none named him but to praise."

     Charley Maxey,
       Sharnbrook.

The end of a working life. Memorial cards of this kind were popular in the period up to 1914. Abner Colson, headmaster of Sharnbrook Council School, died suddenly of heart failure in August 1908, leaving a widow and five children.

Home time. Workers pour out of the Elstow Road factories in Bedford in the late 1950s.

Acknowledgements

The publication of this book would not have been possible without the support of many people and organizations. I would particularly like to thank, on behalf of Bedfordshire Record Office, the many people listed below who have donated or loaned photographs to our collections over the years and without whom this volume would not have been possible. I am also grateful for the help I have received in compiling some of the captions. My special thanks go to my colleagues at the record office for their help and encouragement during the production of the volume.

Mr D. Armstrong • Mrs M. Armstrong • Biggleswade History Society
Mr G.W. Blackburn • Mr W.T. Brantom • Brown and Merry Estate Agents
Mr D.F. Burchmore of The Airship Heritage Trust, Cardington
Mr J.D. Chew • Andrew Clark • Mr J.E. Clark • Mr J. Clarke
Harold G. Clements • Mr M.G. Cole • Mr D.W. Cree • Geoff Dillingham
Mrs E.A. Eastwood • Mrs F.M. Frost • Greene King (Biggleswade) Ltd
Mr D. Hardwick • Hitchin Museum • Colin Holmes • Mrs F. Hopkins
Barry Inskip • Mrs J.M. Johnson • Mr P.M. Kaminski • Mr D. Kitchener
Mr T.B. Kitchener • Bill Knight • Mrs F. Langford • Tom Lawson
Mr A.R. Mossman • NEI Allen Ltd, Bedford • Mr K. Nutting • Mr N. Pacey
Mrs E. Quenby • Mr Jack Read • Mr F. Richards
Ridgmont Baptist Church archives • Mrs D. Rix
Royal Anglian Regiment archives • Mr D.M. Rump • Mrs L. Sabey
Mrs O.V. Skevington • Mr H.G. Smith • Mrs M. Stevens • Mr L. Stevenson
Mr R.A. Taylor • Cyril Tilling • Totternhoe Lime and Stone Co. Ltd.
Andrew Underwood • Mrs M. Wade-Gery • John Wainwright
Mr S. Whitbread • Richard Wildman • Mrs L. Worker

BRITAIN IN OLD PHOTOGRAPHS

To order any of these titles please telephone 0453 731114

ALDERNEY

Alderney: A Second Selection, *B Bonnard*

BEDFORDSHIRE

Bedfordshire at Work, *N Lutt*

BERKSHIRE

Maidenhead, *M Hayles & D Hedges*
Around Maidenhead, *M Hayles & B Hedges*
Reading, *P Southerton*
Reading: A Second Selection, *P Southerton*
Sandhurst and Crowthorne, *K Dancy*
Around Slough, *J Hunter & K Hunter*
Around Thatcham, *P Allen*
Around Windsor, *B Hedges*

BUCKINGHAMSHIRE

Buckingham and District, *R Cook*
High Wycombe, *R Goodearl*
Around Stony Stratford, *A Lambert*

CHESHIRE

Cheshire Railways, *M Hitches*
Chester, *S Nichols*

CLWYD

Clwyd Railways, *M Hitches*

CLYDESDALE

Clydesdale, *Lesmahagow Parish Historical Association*

CORNWALL

Cornish Coast, *T Bowden*
Falmouth, *P Gilson*
Lower Fal, *P Gilson*
Around Padstow, *M McCarthy*
Around Penzance, *J Holmes*
Penzance and Newlyn, *J Holmes*
Around Truro, *A Lyne*
Upper Fal, *P Gilson*

CUMBERLAND

Cockermouth and District, *J Bernard Bradbury*
Keswick and the Central Lakes, *J Marsh*
Around Penrith, *F Boyd*
Around Whitehaven, *H Fancy*

DERBYSHIRE

Derby, *D Buxton*
Around Matlock, *D Barton*

DEVON

Colyton and Seaton, *T Gosling*
Dawlish and Teignmouth, *G Gosling*
Devon Aerodromes, *K Saunders*
Exeter, *P Thomas*
Exmouth and Budleigh Salterton, *T Gosling*
From Haldon to Mid-Dartmoor, *T Hall*
Honiton and the Otter Valley, *J Yallop*
Around Kingsbridge, *K Tanner*
Around Seaton and Sidmouth, *T Gosling*
Seaton, Axminster and Lyme Regis, *T Gosling*

DORSET

Around Blandford Forum, *B Cox*
Bournemouth, *M Colman*
Bridport and the Bride Valley, *J Burrell & S Humphries*
Dorchester, *T Gosling*
Around Gillingham, *P Crocker*

DURHAM

Darlington, *G Flynn*
Darlington: A Second Selection, *G Flynn*
Durham People, *M Richardson*
Houghton-le-Spring and Hetton-le-Hole, *K Richardson*
Houghton-le-Spring and Hetton-le-Hole:
   A Second Selection, *K Richardson*
Sunderland, *S Miller & B Bell*
Teesdale, *D Coggins*
Teesdale: A Second Selection, *P Raine*
Weardale, *J Crosby*
Weardale: A Second Selection, *J Crosby*

DYFED

Aberystwyth and North Ceredigion,
   Dyfed Cultural Services Dept
Haverfordwest, *Dyfed Cultural Services Dept*
Upper Tywi Valley, *Dyfed Cultural Services Dept*

ESSEX

Around Grays, *B Evans*

GLOUCESTERSHIRE

Along the Avon from Stratford to Tewkesbury, *J Jeremiah*
Cheltenham: A Second Selection, *R Whiting*
Cheltenham at War, *P Gill*
Cirencester, *J Welsford*
Around Cirencester, *E Cuss & P Griffiths*
Forest, The, *D Mullin*
Gloucester, *J Voyce*
Around Gloucester, *A Sutton*
Gloucester: From the Walwin Collection, *J Voyce*
North Cotswolds, *D Viner*
Severn Vale, *A Sutton*
Stonehouse to Painswick, *A Sutton*
Stroud and the Five Valleys, *S Gardiner & L Padin*
Stroud and the Five Valleys: A Second Selection,
   S Gardiner & L Padin
Stroud's Golden Valley, *S Gardiner & L Padin*
Stroudwater and Thames & Severn Canals,
   E Cuss & S Gardiner
Stroudwater and Thames & Severn Canals: A Second
   Selection, *E Cuss & S Gardiner*
Tewkesbury and the Vale of Gloucester, *C Hilton*
Thornbury to Berkeley, *J Hudson*
Uley, Dursley and Cam, *A Sutton*
Wotton-under-Edge to Chipping Sodbury, *A Sutton*

GWYNEDD

Anglesey, *M Hitches*
Gwynedd Railways, *M Hitches*
Around Llandudno, *M Hitches*
Vale of Conwy, *M Hitches*

HAMPSHIRE

Gosport, *J Sadden*
Portsmouth, *P Rogers & D Francis*

HEREFORDSHIRE

Herefordshire, *A Sandford*

HERTFORDSHIRE

Barnet, *I Norrie*
Hitchin, *A Fleck*
St Albans, *S Mullins*
Stevenage, *M Appleton*

ISLE OF MAN

The Tourist Trophy, *B Snelling*

ISLE OF WIGHT

Newport, *D Parr*
Around Ryde, *D Parr*

JERSEY

Jersey: A Third Selection, *R Lemprière*

KENT

Bexley, *M Scott*
Broadstairs and St Peter's, *J Whyman*
Bromley, Keston and Hayes, *M Scott*
Canterbury: A Second Selection, *D Butler*
Chatham and Gillingham, *P MacDougall*
Chatham Dockyard, *P MacDougall*
Deal, *J Broady*
Early Broadstairs and St Peter's, *B Wootton*
East Kent at War, *D Collyer*
Eltham, *J Kennett*
Folkestone: A Second Selection, *A Taylor & E Rooney*
Goudhurst to Tenterden, *A Guilmant*
Gravesend, *R Hiscock*
Around Gravesend, *R Hiscock & D Grierson*
Herne Bay, *J Hawkins*
Lympne Airport, *D Collyer*
Maidstone, *I Hales*
Margate, *R Clements*
RAF Hawkinge, *R Humphreys*
RAF Manston, *RAF Manston History Club*
RAF Manston: A Second Selection,
   RAF Manston History Club
Ramsgate and Thanet Life, *D Perkins*
Romney Marsh, *E Carpenter*
Sandwich, *C Wanostrocht*
Around Tonbridge, *C Bell*
Tunbridge Wells, *M Rowlands & I Beavis*
Tunbridge Wells: A Second Selection,
   M Rowlands & I Beavis
Around Whitstable, *C Court*
Wingham, Adisham and Littlebourne, *M Crane*

LANCASHIRE

Around Barrow-in-Furness, *J Garbutt & J Marsh*
Blackpool, *C Rothwell*
Bury, *J Hudson*
Chorley and District, *J Smith*
Fleetwood, *C Rothwell*
Heywood, *J Hudson*
Around Kirkham, *C Rothwell*
Lancashire North of the Sands, *J Garbutt & J Marsh*
Around Lancaster, *S Ashworth*
Lytham St Anne's, *C Rothwell*
North Fylde, *C Rothwell*
Radcliffe, *J Hudson*
Rossendale, *B Moore & N Dunnachie*

LEICESTERSHIRE

Around Ashby-de-la-Zouch, *K Hillier*
Charnwood Forest, *I Keil, W Humphrey & W Wix*
Leicester, *D Burton*
Leicester: A Second Selection, *D Burton*
Melton Mowbray, *T Hickman*
Around Melton Mowbray, *T Hickman*
River Soar, *D Wix, P Shacklock & I Keil*
Rutland, *T Clough*
Vale of Belvoir, *T Hickman*
Around the Welland Valley, *S Mastoris*

LINCOLNSHIRE

Grimsby, *J Tierney*
Around Grimsby, *J Tierney*
Grimsby Docks, *J Tierney*
Lincoln, *D Cuppleditch*